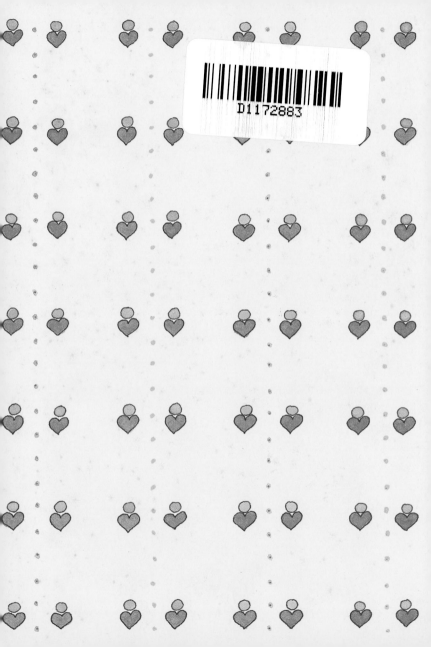

To: JACOB's MOTHER

From: RED

# Babies Take Us On A Special Journey

by
Susan Squellati Florence

The C.R. Gibson Company, Norwalk, Ct. 06856

Babies take us
on a special journey
into the land of love.

They bring us
to a place
that we never knew
existed...

but was always there
inside...
just waiting for a child
to open the door.

This is the place
where loving begins...

and we find
that by giving
we become full.

Babies bring us back
to our own small
beginnings.

Knowing we were once
so small and dependent,
we meet the child in us.

We see
our parents
in a new way...

and know how much
we mean to them.

Babies bring us
to a new awareness.

Many things we took
for granted become
small wonders:

the wonder of growing ...
of moving ...
of touching ...

and smiling!

Babies teach us
many things:

that order is not as
stimulating as messes...

that schedules
　　　　are flexible...

that there is
　　　　no such thing
as a full night's sleep.

Most of all,
we learn that time
(which is so precious to us)
means nothing
to our baby.

We touch...
and hug...
and hold...
and rock gently...
as time stands still.

And we know,
without a single word,
the love that exists
between us. ♡

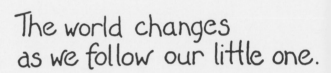

The world changes
as we follow our little one.

We pause
to watch a bug crawl by...
a butterfly soar...
and a frog leap.

We find that puddles
   are for stepping in...
      not over

that lawns feel good
      under bare feet...

and worms are fun
         to hold!

There will be times
when you wonder
why you ever
took this journey...

where too much
is expected of you ...

where the tug and pull
and demands on your time
leave you
tired
and
frustrated.

This is the time
to stop
to listen to yourself...
to fill your own needs...
to take a break...
to ask for help.

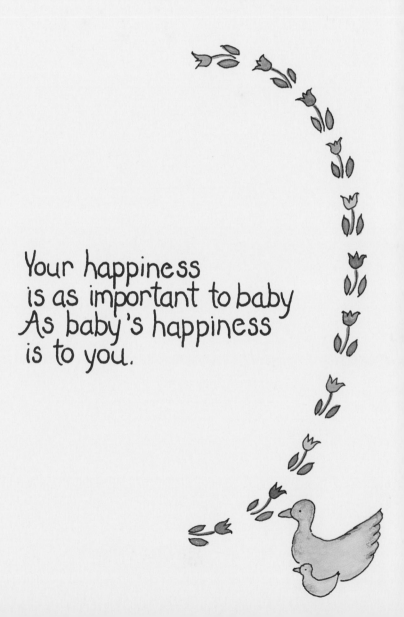

Your happiness
is as important to baby
As baby's happiness
is to you.

With the years,
your baby
will grow...

and as mother
or father
all the care,
and nurturing,
and time
you have given
will not be needed.

But what your child
will always need
is the love
you've shared.

This endless circle
of love returned
will always nurture
your child.

Babies take us
on a special journey...

to the land of love
within our hearts.

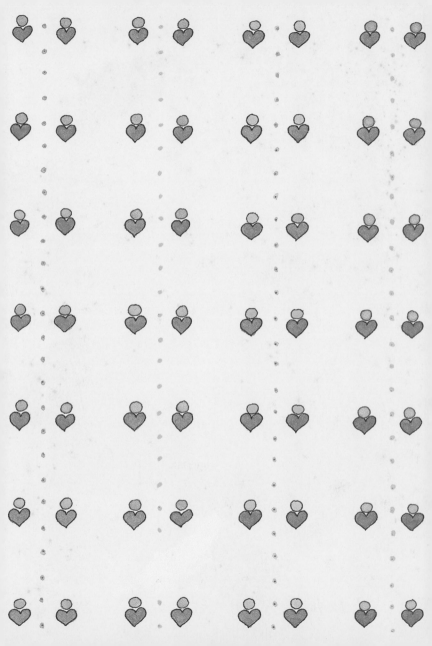